Corporate Strategies for Effective Communications

Edited by Theresa Brothers and Holly Gallo

Contents

5   FROM THE PRESIDENT

6   EXECUTIVE SUMMARY

Part I

7   YOUR COMPANY'S FIRST AND FOREMOST COMMUNICATOR
J.P. Donlon
Chief Executive Magazine

9   HELPFUL TIPS ON HIRING A CONSULTANT
Robert B. Wolcott, Jr.
Braun Ketchum Public Relations

11   THE THREE "I's" OF COMMUNICATIONS
Edward M. Stanton
Manning, Selvage & Lee

12   THE 10-STEP COMMUNICATIONS PLAN
Lester R. Potter, ABC
Towers Perrin–Washington Consulting Office

13   MEASURING THE EFFECTIVENESS OF THE COMMUNICATIONS PROGRAM
Brad Whitworth
Hewlett-Packard Company

15   MONITORING THE EFFECTIVENESS OF A COMPANY-WIDE PRODUCTION
Jeffrey Goldstein
Merck & Company, Inc.

Part II

17   CREATIVE METHODS TO GAIN MEDIA ATTENTION
George B. McGrath
Osgood Global Group

19   PLANNING AND CARRYING OUT THE STRATEGY
James R. Allen
Consolidated Freightways, Inc.

21   DELIVERING A STRATEGIC BLUEPRINT FOR RESULTS
Diane C. Siegel
First Interstate Bancorp

23 BUILDING CREDIBILITY FOR INCREASED PRODUCTIVITY
Nelson Farris
Nike, Inc.

25 DESIGNING A SUCCESSFUL VIDEO PROGRAM
Catherine Chuplis
Levi Strauss & Company

Part III

27 MANAGING THE COMMUNICATIONS PROCESS
Phyllis Piano
General Electric Medical Systems

29 CAN WE INFLUENCE EUROPEAN GOVERNMENTS?
Andrew A. Napier
Ford of Europe, Inc.

31 ORGANIZING CROSS-CULTURAL COMMUNICATIONS
Thomas Henderson
Dow Europe S.A.

33 EMPLOYEE COMMUNICATIONS ACROSS CULTURAL BORDERS
Felix Bjorklund
IBM Europe S.A.

35 THE CHANGING WORLD AND SATELLITE COMMUNICATIONS
Bruce L. Crockett
COMSAT Corporation

Part IV

37 ATTEMPTED MERGER AT SOUTHERN CALIFORNIA EDISON
Lewis M. Phelps
Southern California Edison Company

39 ADDRESSING SAFETY AND ENVIRONMENTAL ISSUES
Thomas Houston
Chrysler Corporation

41 COMMUNICATIONS' ROLE IN REDEFINING A CULTURE
Richard M. Madden
Allstate Insurance Company

42 MOLDING COMMUNICATIONS TO THE ORGANIZATION
Tricia E. Palermo
Pacific Telesis Group

44 SENDING A POSITIVE MESSAGE DURING DIFFICULT TIMES
Terrence D. Straub
USX Corporation

From the President

The growing interest in corporate communications is an indicator of the quickening pace of both domestic and international business. Supporting the CEO's vision and values, sharing information with all employees, and getting facts out to the public are all increasingly important parts of the communications function.

Two Board conferences—Strategies for Effective Corporate Communications, held in Los Angeles, and Cross Border Corporate Communications, held in Paris—addressed these issues. This report presents highlights of the valuable experiences shared by the executives who spoke.

The Board would like to thank the many executives who participated in these conferences. We are particularly grateful to the contributors to this report.

PRESTON TOWNLEY
President and CEO

Executive Summary

Many changes have occurred in the corporate communications function in recent years. Internally, the growing emphasis on quality through employee buy-in, stepped-up production requirements, and widespread organizational change have increased the importance of daily corporate communications. Externally, corporate communicators are attempting to keep the media abreast of corporate activity, but it is now harder to "get a message out." Moreover, companies are expecting higher returns on their communications dollars.

A major theme of this report is how to more effectively manage the communications function. Lester Potter of Towers Perrin outlines a 10-step guide for creating a strategic plan for corporate communications, and two executives, one from Hewlett-Packard and a second from Merck & Company, offer advice on measuring the effectiveness of communications. A consultant from Braun Ketchum Public Relations gives some tips on hiring a public relations firm.

J.P. Donlon of *Chief Executive Magazine,* as well as many other speakers, asserts that corporate communications is much aided by top executive support, particularly a CEO who takes time to talk openly with both employees and the media. In fact, says Donlon, open communications is your CEO's only communications option today. Terrence Straub presented USX's Chairman, Chuck Corry, as an example for others to follow.

In internal communications, the most effective mechanisms are tailored to individual corporate cultures. For example, Nike uses an informal approach to communications which matches its approach to business, including brown-bag lunches, news briefs, and special events to suit the mood of the employees. Levi Strauss & Co. wants to build a learning organization, and it sees a future in interactive video, where employees can get as much or as little information as they want. To prepare for this future, Levi Strauss & Co. is working on introducing this technology in today's workplace. First Interstate Bancorp has found the more traditional face-to-face meetings with executives to be the most effective way to transmit information and bind everyone to a common culture.

In global companies, communicating internally—disseminating information quickly and efficiently and linking employees to a common corporate culture—becomes even more difficult. Language barriers and cultural differences are but two of the hindrances to cross-border communications mentioned by executives from Dow Europe, General Electric Medical Systems, Ford of Europe, and IBM Europe. Some possible solutions are presented, but all concede that there is no "quick fix." Bruce Crockett, President and CEO of COMSAT, explains the role satellites may eventually play in cross-cultural communications.

While internal communications are becoming more important, companies are also interested in maintaining open external communications, particularly with the media. A consultant, George McGrath from Osgood Global Group, shares ideas on how to gain media attention. And Consolidated Freightways provides a case study in how this diversified transportation company successfully "advertised" its revolutionary image processing system.

When crises occur, both internal and external communications assume a more visible role. Some crises are obvious, such as the media battle Southern California Edison endured or the environmental headaches left to Chrysler Corporation. Others are more subtle but equally pressing: The change in corporate culture at Allstate Insurance and Pacific Telesis' need to create its own culture after the break-up of AT&T both presented unique communications experiences with valuable lessons.

In general, there was some consensus among speakers. Serious attention to communications—through goal-setting, utilization of all possible media (both new and tried-and-true), and consistent, candid messages—appears to be the best way to build employer-employee relationships and communicate effectively with people outside of corporations.

Part I

Your Company's First and Foremost Communicator

J.P. Donlon
Editor in Chief
Chief Executive Magazine

The question of communicating is intrinsically bound to the notion of leadership both as the leader himself sees it and as those serving him see it. In his forthcoming book, *A Briefing for Leaders*, Bob Dillenschneider, former Hill & Knowlton CEO, raises four important questions for leaders and potential leaders that relate to the communication issue:

- What must I be?
- What reality must I work in?
- What are my tools?
- What are my worthwhile goals, and how can they be reached?

As a professional communicator, you must help your chief executive answer these questions.

A Brief History

In the 1950s and 1960s, power and leadership were exercised through administrative control. Conformity and hierarchy, often leading to inflexibility and rigidity, communicated a leader's power and his vision of the enterprise. The great conglomerateurs such as ITT's Harold Geneen, United Technology's Harry Gray, Gulf & Western's Charlie Bluhdorn, and CBS's Bill Paley communicated their vision through sheer size or entrepreneurial audacity. Once when Paley entered a management meeting and sat at one of the middle seats at a long boardroom table, a young executive asked Paley if he would prefer to sit at the head of the table. Paley stared at the fellow and said dryly, "Young man, wherever I happen to sit *is* the head of the table."

In the 1970s and 1980s, leadership became synonymous with exception-driven management. CEOs ceased being custodians and exerted power through fundamental restructuring. Whatever interfered with the goals of market-driven management was unsentimentally tossed. Remember Jack Welsh's dictum of the 1980s: "GE will either be number one or number two in each of its markets, or it won't be in that market." GE managers and employees certainly go that message: 80,000 fewer people are employed at GE today.

After an era of restructuring and consolidation, mergers and acquisitions, the glue that once adhered people to organizations fails to bind. People are no longer inclined to accept a Geneen or Paley style of leadership, whatever the talents or skills that may be on offer.

Honesty as the CEO's Primary Tool

The 1990s are becoming the age of internal and external communications. In my encounters with chief executives, nearly all assert that they value their people highly. How many times have you heard this expression: "Our company's most important assets go down the elevator every day?" How many references to "our team" or "our dedicated family of employees" have you read in annual reports or company literature? Yet, how many of your managers and employees believe this? Do you believe it? My point is that in the 1990s trust is your CEO's only path to communicate effectively both within the organization and to the outside world.

You're probably thinking this is obvious, yet consider what the employees at Salomon thought when its CEO was revealed to have known about illegal treasury market transactions. Never mind the employees. The grandson of the firm's founder told *The New York Times* that he even considered removing his family name from the door and changing the company name.

Let's set aside cases of wrongdoing, which are few in number. Many companies do business honestly every day. What about the honest chief executive, obsessed by leaks, who sends eager-to-please officers to flush out the aide who is telling *The Wall Street Journal* reporter about internal shakeups and plans? After weeks of stonewalling reporters and issuing "no impropriety here" press releases, Procter & Gamble's CEO repented. But casting suspicion on present and former employees in this fashion did nothing to communicate P&G's belief in its people. The gulf of trust that ordinarily divides a leader from his group suddenly becomes an ocean.

People thirst for leadership yet are suspicious of leaders. Charisma, the false god of leadership, engenders mistrust today. Management expert Peter Drucker calls it a trap, the undoing of leaders, because it encourages inflexibility and resistance to change.

Using the Truth to Bind Employees

Since CEOs must work in the reality of apprehension and skepticism, they must display openness and deal honestly. Simple and direct tools are needed; accessibility is the greatest asset.

Home Depot's Bernie Marcus has a quarterly "town meeting" with employees. Held in a given store, linked by satellite, and beamed into all stores across the United States, these Sunday breakfasts are casual affairs. He tells everyone Home Depot's plans: Why it expects to expand into one area and not another; why it may want to carry one line of product but not another. He reserves time at the end of every meeting for fielding any question from any employee anywhere in the country.

If a CEO has only one strategic goal as a leader, it ought to be to communicate his vision of the company to his employees. Corporate leaders who believe their time can be better spent on more tangible issues (production, marketing or technology) may want to rethink their priorities. In a survey of 500 CEOs and presidents, clear strategic intent was cited as the number one *factor* for achieving global competitive excellence. The overwhelming critical competitive *resources* are people and talent. The obvious conclusion is that CEOs today must communicate that strategic intent to the one resource that will make it happen—people.

My central point is that all competitive advantages today are short-lived. Technology? Your rivals are already working on new and better systems. Capital? Well, hardly; in a global market capital moves overnight to where the higher returns are. Distribution? Forget it! Market franchises are made and unmade every week. The key to the 1990s is that understanding and buy-in are necessary to win.

Helpful Tips on Hiring a Consultant

Robert B. Wolcott, Jr.
Senior Consultant
Braun Ketchum Public Relations

If you believe that you require the services of an agency, how do you get started? I believe that the job begins with you, the prospective client.

The Initial Meeting

Bring a lot of basic information to the initial meeting with a potential agency. Figure out your needs and wants, and how you can convey your company's mission and nature to the agency so it can respond more effectively. That saves considerable time for both parties.

In the first discussion, you should indicate your company's internal public relations capabilities. Often an agency will initially be invited to audit an existing program. Sometimes the director of public relations orders those audits to assess the firm's strengths and weaknesses, to identify areas of redundancy, or to reconfirm an "insider" opinion of internal capabilities and deficiencies.

You'll certainly want to tell the agency the nature of the job. Is it a project, a one-time deal? Is there a rough budget? Is it local, national or international? Later, this forms a basis to evaluate an agency's capabilities.

Look at the agency's client list. If they don't want to show you that list, beware. A good client list is an agency's best testimonial. Ask how long the agency has had each of its clients; that tells you something about client turnover. You want an agency with a good client retention record because it can help reveal their proficiency and competence. Ask to look at last year's client list, and compare it with the current list. Don't hesitate to ask for names of former clients as references; sometimes an ex-client can be as praising as a present client.

Proposals and Price

When you're done talking, they'll give you their "sales pitch." The agency will usually tell you its size, history, number of offices, track record, number of professionals by various categories of expertise, and so on. Some very large agencies will tell you that they've got whatever you want, wherever you want it. That may or may not be true. A smaller, specialized agency can sometimes do a much better job.

If you've given them enough information about what you need, what your problems are, where the company stands today, what you would like to achieve, and what the goals and target audiences are, you should expect some kind of response. I would be leery of a very detailed, in-depth proposal with many specific recommendations. Nobody can be that knowledgeable about a company in a single meeting. On the other hand, the agency should provide a few suggestions for a program to give you an idea of how they approach a problem, need, or continuing communications requirement.

They should also provide a rough cost estimate. You shouldn't pin them down precisely, but it should tell you the "ballpark figure" and its basis. Some agencies will charge a monthly or annual retainer, which is supposed to cover everything. Many firms charge a minimum plus hours actually incurred on behalf of the client. Some will simply operate on an hourly charge with some cap so that the meter isn't running amok. You ought to find out how an agency charges and how they keep track of their time.

These questions may sound picky, but they get to the heart of the firm—their business acumen as well as their professionalism. Do they mark up expenses, charge commissions, or bill everything net? These are questions you need to ask before starting a relationship.

Up front, you must set some measuring standards, some indices that you can turn to a year later to evaluate the work done by the agency. If you haven't set up those yardsticks, you won't be able to complain that you didn't get your money's worth.

Mutual respect is critical. If the president of the agency makes the big pitch to you, ask to meet the person who will actually handle your account. You should meet separately with that person and evaluate the chemistry between the two of you. You should also find out if you'll ever see the president again. Even in a large agency, you ought to feel that the leader cares about your business, will continue to be interested in it, and will occasionally talk to you.

In summary, choosing an agency is not quite like entering matrimony, but it does require a lot of tender loving care.

The Three "I's" of Communications

Edward M. Stanton
Chairman
Manning, Selvage & Lee

When I was a feature writer, the editor of a paper wanted me to do an article on success. I found general agreement among people I interviewed on one word that described their secret to success; that word was "involvement." Since it begins with an "I," this leads me to what I call the "Three I's" of successful strategy for a dynamic company: involvement, imagination and imitation.

Involvement

People don't usually want to get involved, but in the communications business, group involvement is a must. For example, one of our clients was the highly regarded Steinway piano company. When the business was sold to CBS, competitors started the rumor that the new Steinway pianos were inferior in quality. We called everybody together—the Steinway brothers, the marketing department, the advertising agency, the technicians—and drew up a battle plan. Part of the plan was to get a story in *The New York Times* about Yamaha. As it happened, the president of Yamaha said that he plays a Steinway because it's the best quality in the world.

Imagination or Innovation

You need to throw away most of the ideas you come up with and try something entirely new and creative. The human mind resists change because it's easier to keep using the same old ideas that seem to work rather than come up with new ideas. For example, we put together a two-year program for Minute Maid targeted at women. The 1984 Olympic Games added the first women's marathon, so we came up with the idea of a cross-country relay marathon for women. Minute Maid told us we were out of our minds and gave us many reasons for not doing it. We fought and finally got the company to agree. It was one of our most successful special events, *and* it sold orange juice.

Imitation

Unfortunately, this word has negative connotations, yet it's one of the most underrated of all business concepts. While it is important to be creative, I contend that you don't always have to reinvent the wheel. Some ideas that have worked are good and should be repeated again and again. If something works for one client, try it with another client.

My remarks have moved from the general to the specific, from framing the three general concepts of involvement, imagination and imitation, and then providing a couple of case histories to illustrate these concepts. I urge you to remember the words of the Greek philosopher Aristotle who wrote, "If you want to appear to be something, then you must first be what you want to appear to be." If your corporation and management want to be perceived as dynamic, progressive and strategically wise, they must first be dynamic, progressive and strategically wise.

The 10-Step Communications Plan

Lester R. Potter, ABC
Consultant, Towers Perrin–
Washington Consulting Office
IABC Chairman, 1991-1992

How do you implement a communications plan? Let the classical corporate strategic plan serve as a guide to its construction. I use a 10-part plan that works whether you're planning an overall annual communications program or whether you're dealing with a single issue.

- First, a good communications plan starts with a communications philosophy. What do you expect from the plan? What do you hope to accomplish?

- Second is a description of the communication process. This serves to train managers who are unfamiliar with communication but whose support is necessary for the plan's success. The idea is to help them understand the process of communication so that they can buy into and support it.

- Third is background. How did you get here, where do you stand, and where are you going? This sets the stage for why the plan is needed. Here's a good place to insert a mission statement or vision and your organization's values. These govern communication regardless of the issues addressed in the plan.

- Fourth is a situation analysis. What are the major issues you face? To do this, put each issue on a separate page and list the facts related to it. Example: "One of our plants is perceived as an extreme polluter." Now list the facts—they might show that you don't pollute. List the issue and the actual facts on which you're going to build your program, using research as a foundation.

- Fifth is the message statement: What do you generally want to communicate?

- Sixth, list the audiences in order of importance.

- Seventh is a one- or two-sentence message you want to get across to each specific audience.

- Eighth is implementation. How will you turn the plan into reality? What are your goals and objectives, strategies, tactics, and action plans to get the plan accomplished? What media/channels will you employ?

- Ninth is the budget, broken down by activity then totaled.

- Tenth is measurement, evaluation and course correction. This is extremely important. For an annual plan, you cannot wait until the end of the year to do your monitoring and evaluation. It's best to get feedback every quarter either formally or informally on your success. If you find you're not accomplishing objects, you can go back and make course corrections so that you have a plan that succeeds.

Strategic thinking can mean greater success for any communications professional because it creates focus. When you continuously monitor, evaluate and make course corrections, you can't fail.

Measuring the Effectiveness of The Communications Program

Brad Whitworth
Public Affairs Manager
Hewlett-Packard Company

Because communications is more art than science, it is often difficult to measure its specific contribution to a final outcome. However, public relations professionals are experiencing increased pressure to show that communications efforts *do* make a difference. There are four major decisions you need to worry about when measuring. Should the research be:

- quantitative or qualitative?
- formal or informal?
- conducted internally or externally?
- focused on the long or short term?

Let me give you examples from Hewlett-Packard to illustrate these dilemmas.

Quantitative vs. Qualitative

When we tried to sell the idea of a video magazine to our senior management team, we had done all our "homework"; for example, we showed what other companies were doing with employee video. With this information, we appealed to the half of the brain which requires quantitative proof. At the same time, we showed a qualitative application story of how Hewlett-Packard computers were being used at Lucas Films to help with the special effects for the *Star Wars* movies. I think the final okay for the video magazine resulted from both the excitement of seeing some of these special effects, realizing that it was our equipment that made it possible, as well as from the more quantitative proof.

Formal vs. Informal

There's also the need for a balance between two other poles: the formal versus the informal. I tend to prefer the informal. A couple of years ago, I used to "brown bag" lunch with groups of employees to get feedback on our communications system. However, we use a more formal approach when analyzing press clippings. Our media relations people use this analysis to find out what percentage of clippings actually convey some of these messages that we are trying to send.

Internal vs. External

Should measuring be done internally or externally? Internally, we recently conducted a functional management communications survey that went to our R&D, manufacturing, marketing and general managers around the world. We were trying to find out how information got to them and whether or not they received senior management messages. Most of the project consisted of a formal questionnaire, but we also made follow-up phone calls.

Balance that with an external measure. We wanted to find out whether our external communications programs were effective. We went to an outside source and asked him to gather information from the trade press, business press and major dailies on how Hewlett-Packard's press relations activities stacked up against our competitors'. It turned out to be heavy on the qualitative, but this was very valuable for continuous improvement purposes. Accordingly, balance is required between the internal focus and the external realities.

Short Term vs. Long Term

Probably the most difficult to balance are short-term versus long-term measures. I'm talking about everything from employee attitude surveys to public opinion surveys to "quick and dirty" questionnaires. There's no denying that public affairs is probably the best equipped to handle reactive situations in an organization. We need to have a vision, but because most of us are deadline- or action-oriented, one of the strengths we bring to an organization is our ability to react.

In trying to develop measures for public affairs, I've been working with our marketing research information center. They put out a report with all kinds of data which proved very interesting for our purposes. One thing we talked about was employee communications: How do you measure its effectiveness? We've determined that you need to do pre/post testing around a specific communications effort to focus on whether it has had any effect in the workplace.

For example, before we launched the video magazine, we did a pre/post test. It was a random control survey with 50 employees as a test group and 50 as the control group. We showed the new video magazine in pilot form to the test group and then asked them a series of questions. We asked the same set of questions of the control group that never saw the video. We found the test group had statistically higher, more positive answers on every question dealing with video content than did the control group. We proved that we could actually change employees' perceptions, attitudes and information bases through exposure to a program.

The bad part about a pre/post test is that you can't be sure whether you're hitting a momentary high, where information won't be retained, or whether you've reached a new plateau. That's why you need a longevity study of some sort to track these people over time. We have a pilot program with people we can survey regularly who know that they're going to be asked a series of questions. Employee attitude surveys are also good longevity studies. If you have a large, broad-based sample over a long period of time, you'll develop a snapshot of what employees, the community or the media are saying about the organization. Again, both a short-term and a long-term perspective are important.

Monitoring the Effectiveness of A Company-Wide Production

Jeffrey Goldstein
Manager, Corporate Communications
Merck & Company, Inc.

Do you always have to monitor the effectiveness of a company-wide production? Not always. However, there are valid reasons for measuring, such as cost and program effectiveness. It can be very useful to know that the money you spent got the message across to its intended audience. In monitoring a program's effectiveness, there's no substitute for a well-planned, well-researched design strategy.

First, define what it is you want to measure because that will affect what strategy you use. Second, define "the client": Who wants to know if the program is effective? The person or department who paid for the program? Top management? Sales or marketing? Knowing who the client is will help you decide what to measure.

If, for example, you want to know how many people watch a video, you can count the number of copies requested, use a sign-in sheet to count the number of people who attend a showing, or assign personnel to count the number of people watching a video at different monitors at various times of day. How you show a video is important for evaluation. It is easy to get feedback from a video shown on company time because a questionnaire can be filled out then and there (see box).

You may also want to know audience response. If you do a program on sexual harassment, you can see whether more complaints on sexual harassment come in. If the topic is safety, you may want to see if the number of lost-time accidents has decreased. You can also

---

Goldstein's Theories of Video Production

- The effectiveness of a video is directly related to how it is shown. It is most effective to show it at staff meetings; it is least effective to have employees view it at home. (They don't like to watch company "propaganda" on their own time.)
- The effectiveness of a video is directly related to how it is distributed. Use your imagination for distribution. Have lending libraries, show it as cable television, or use other innovative methods.
- The effectiveness of a video is related to whether print material supplements the video; this can include booklets for training, print publications for employee information, posters, and brochures.
- The effectiveness of a video depends on how important the information is to the viewer. Will it affect employees' lives or how well they do their jobs?
- The effectiveness of a video depends on how well it is designed, not necessarily how much it costs. That requires well-defined objectives and messages as well as material that is well-written, shot and edited. For example, if a video is to be viewed on the employees' own time, you may want to add more entertainment, drama or humor.
- Before you measure the success of a program, define success. Make sure the client knows what to expect and has realistic goals. Ask yourself and your client *why* you're doing the video, *whom* it is for, *what* are the two or three key messages, and *how* you want the viewer to respond.

measure how well a new procedure is learned by finding out, for example, whether or not the new medical benefits forms are being filled out correctly.

Creating a Questionnaire

It is harder to measure knowledge of an issue or attitude change. To measure these, you need questionnaires or focus groups.

How you construct a questionnaire depends on what you want to measure. Some questionnaires give respondents five choices; others require simple yes or no answers. One tip: If a video is being shown at a meeting, have the meeting leader fill out a questionnaire to assess the group's reaction. You can often learn something from an outside, objective viewpoint.

When doing a questionnaire, look carefully at how you've written the questions. Ask yourself:

1. Are the questions neutral, or do they lead the respondent?
2. Are the questions simple and easy to understand?
3. Are the questions double-barreled? For example, if you pose a question like "Is this program balanced and objective?" you are asking too much at once. It may be one and not the other, and the respondent's true answer may be obscured.
4. Do you allow for open-ended reaction?
5. Do you try to use humor?
6. Have you pre-tested your questionnaire?

How you distribute and collect the questionnaire is important. Try to make it an enclosure of some sort, and include a phone or fax number for people who may feel more comfortable responding in these ways. Follow-up is very important; don't send your questionnaires into a vacuum. Use the phone, and actively seek results. It's very important to reach people who don't watch the program or who don't like the program because you can learn from them.

Other Forms of Measuring

Focus-group testing is an excellent idea, both before and after you distribute the program, and it is absolutely critical if you're designing a new program. Otherwise, you might be giving the wrong message to an unreceptive audience. It's also good to post-test for feedback and to see if you've overlooked anything. I don't recommend showing rough cuts because people have a hard time understanding them.

Focus-group testing also allows the audience to express opinions. Use representative samples of your entire target audience, including supervisors and employees, blue- and white-collar workers. Since focus-group testing isn't as scientific as questionnaires, the information tends to be more anecdotal, but you may gather information that wouldn't come out in a more formal questionnaire. It's good practice to use both methods.

My company does a company-wide attitude survey every two years. It measures employees' attitudes about issues such as physical working conditions, pay, as well as the cost of pharmaceuticals; it also measures how employees feel about company publications. If such a survey exists in your company, take advantage of it to measure the effectiveness of your ongoing and recent programs.

Another way to check the effectiveness of your communications is a company-wide communications audit. Usually done by an outside consultant, it is very useful for measuring print as well as video productions.

Part II

Creative Methods to Gain Media Attention

George B. McGrath
Senior Counselor
Osgood Global Group

There are several ways you can gain attention for your company in the media: Ask the CEO to run away with his or her secretary, invite an environmental group to blockade the gates to your plant, or discover an accounting error that will totally throw off your quarterly earnings. Actually, I want to talk about creatively "selling" your company's story to the press.

Why do we have to "sell" the press our news? Because we have a big challenge in persuading the media that we've got something interesting to talk about. For one, there have been severe cutbacks in media staff over the last few years. Newspapers are contracting, leaving fewer ad pages and less editorial space. Therefore, you must "sell" a story about your company's product or service.

Story Segmentation

To sell a story, you need to look for ways to personalize your information to the needs of the target publication or broadcast media. Get well-acquainted with the publications you're sending to, and find a way to fit the story into the publication. This approach is called "story segmentation."

For example, a few years ago B.F. Goodrich had just gone through a corporate restructuring, which shifted its focus to plastics and aerospace components. But they were still best known for tires. They wanted to get attention for their successful restructuring and financial turnaround, so they came up with an ideal story: a corporate profile of a company in transition. B.F. Goodrich is a name-brand company, and the story made a classic case study for the Sunday newspaper's business section.

How did Goodrich further segment the story? The editorial page editor of *The Wall Street Journal* talked with the CEO on what goes through a CEO's mind when he's trying to keep one step ahead of corporate raiders. The result was a think piece in *The Journal's* "Business World" column on the challenges involved in corporate restructuring from a CEO's viewpoint.

Then, Goodrich focused on the high-tech aerospace segment of its business. They talked to reporters who covered aerospace, telling them how Goodrich was developing carbon-brake technology for aircraft.

In addition, the company went to a well-known syndicated columnist and suggested a story about companies that are really best known for products they no longer produce. It made a fun feature column and Goodrich was mentioned as an example of a company best known for its tire business but now involved in many other high-tech areas, including specialty chemicals and aerospace.

In each case, Goodrich targeted and personalized its approach to the media. They developed variations on the turnaround and restructuring story to suit a broad range of media, from Op-Ed pieces to the trade magazine stories. And the company laid the groundwork for media relationships that would serve it well in the future.

Three Other Tactics for Promoting Your Company

Another way to get media attention is to identify areas of expertise within your company which would be helpful to reporters. Produce a Rolodex card that identifies people in the company who are experts on certain technical areas or issues, and mail the card to a journalist who may be covering these subjects. You probably know people within your own company who can be useful resources.

One proven tactic to leverage your expertise is surveys and polls on hot topics. Naturally, there must be a reasonable link to your company. Dun & Bradstreet, for example, issues regular outlooks on the economic trends generated from information gathered from corporate purchasing managers. To promote its allergy medication line, a pharmaceutical company compiles an allergy index based on forecasts of allergists in 35 metropolitan areas. When hay fever season comes around, newspapers and radio stations look for this information. To be most effective, these types of polls or information services must be maintained over a period of time.

Getting caught doing good never hurt, either. Do something beneficial for society and get caught doing it. With today's increased focus on corporate ethics and corporate social responsibility, it makes good sense to make this part of your media relations effort.

Recently, Continental Airlines was seeking ways to gain attention for their new service to Frankfurt, Germany. On the surface, it was a simple trade story, but the new route was very important to Continental because they had an opportunity to break into a major market. Because of their financial situation, they had limited funds for advertising, so they developed a program to draw media attention. At the end of the Persian Gulf war, many U.S. military personnel couldn't afford to fly home to see their families before going back to German bases. So Continental earmarked 100 seats on its inaugural flight to Frankfurt to reunite stateside families with the troops in Germany on Father's Day weekend. The company worked with local television stations and veterans group in 14 markets to distribute those seats. The program developed into a rich and wonderful human interest story that received national coverage.

I challenge you to look for creative ways to extend your media relations efforts. Seek something new and different. There's a great need for that type of story.

Planning and Carrying Out the Strategy

James R. Allen
Vice President, Public Relations
Consolidated Freightways, Inc.

Consolidated Freightways is a diversified transportation holding company in Palo Alto, California. We have 11 revenue companies that operate under three basic groups: Consolidated Freightways Motorfreight, our long-haul, national trucking company; Conway Transportation Services, our regional and short-haul trucking; and Emery Worldwide, our air freight company. In 1991, we'll achieve about $4.5 billion in revenue from 45,000 employees who work in more than 1,500 freight facilities in 88 countries around the world.

At Consolidated, planning is very important. Why have a plan? For one thing, it is essential to achieving a goal. Even more important, it can keep bad things from happening. Any plan should be logical, results-oriented, meaningful and specific. Let me give you an example of how we successfully launched a new product using these rules.

Consolidated Freightways recently developed a remarkable image processing system. Before image processing came on line, if a customer wanted to see documentation on whether a shipment arrived, it would take about seven days to process the paperwork. With image processing, when the customer calls for documentation, an employee calls the scan document up on a screen, types in the fax number of the customer, pushes a button, and the customer receives the documentation in a matter of seconds. We're the first trucking company to use this system.

Setting Goals and Anticipating Challenges

Presenting the national media with a true technological innovation was the challenge. Public relations and marketing had several goals in getting this story into the marketplace. We wanted to highlight the advantages of the image processing system to our customers, and we wanted to reach potential buyers of the system's application because we have a marketing agreement with our joint venture partner on the resale of these systems.

Next, we anticipated what could stop us from achieving these goals. The first thing was to convince senior management, which wasn't a hard sell in this instance. A more challenging dilemma was publicizing the system during the Gulf war. We had to make the decision whether to move forward with it or hold back, not knowing when the war was going to end. We opted to move forward.

We also had to cope with the recession's effect on the news media. There's less advertising in magazines and newspapers, and as a result, there's less editorial space. The "news well" is smaller, and therefore it's more challenging for companies like us to get our story told in those papers.

Next, we had to contend with the fact that Consolidated Freightways is not a household name. How do you associate a trucking company with technology? This hurdle actually became a strength which we used to our advantage. In addition, we had to simplify extremely technical subject matter for the media. And we wanted to localize our announcement: If you're the business editor of a paper in a small town in Pennsylvania, it's easy to throw away a press release from a company in California. We had to work to overcome that.

Finally, we wanted to be able to convey our innovation to the trucking industry first so that we could position ourselves from a competitive standpoint.

The Execution Phase

Since we didn't have the in-house capability to reach our desired audience, we hired a public relations agency. We worked with them to produce clear, concise media materials. Our sales and media materials had to be personalized so that our three divisions would receive the benefit—not some holding company in Palo Alto.

Getting your story told in *The New York Times* is a great way to make you and your CEO feel good. But part of our plan was to achieve new business from an innovation, so getting our story told in small, local papers was also very important. This way, the local sales reps could show their customers the stories from the local papers.

Taking into consideration the visual impact of *U.S.A. Today's* graphic treatments on American newspapers, we wanted to be right in there and make our story easier to use by the media. We hired the graphic arts director for *The L.A. Times* and paid him on a freelance basis to develop our graphics just as if he were on an assignment from his employer. He did an excellent job, and the graphics had a usage percentage of well over 60 percent.

Now for the pitch. To appeal to editors, we emphasized the industry-first application and the customer-focused benefits, making this story seem less self-serving to Consolidated Freightways. Finally, we highlighted the potential applications of this innovation in many businesses, not just the trucking industry. Not only did we target the traditional trade magazines but also the publications that our customers read every day.

The results were very pleasing, and we met our objectives: We got key national clips and appeared in the smaller papers. In addition, we had some unexpected results from our campaign. We received inquiries from other transportation businesses outside the trucking industry. More important, we had about 12 requests from customers not in the trucking or transportation business who wanted to apply our system to their businesses. Right now, several sales are pending on this system.

In a word, the success of the strategy can actually be predetermined by a well thought-out plan. Proper planning for a media campaign builds in success before the program even gets to the point of execution. Failures occur from improper focus and from failing to address the three common sense rules: Was it logical? Was it meaningful and specific? And did it properly anticipate results?

Delivering a Strategic Blueprint for Results

Diane C. Siegel
Senior Vice President, Internal Communications
Special Events & Executive Services
First Interstate Bancorp

We've all had days when the profit motive wasn't motive enough. When this happens in corporate affairs, we look to communications to provide the glue that binds employees to the corporation; to show them the overall corporate purpose and how they, as individuals, fit into it. Surveys show managers as the premier "applicators" of that glue. Whether it's your own manager or a senior executive, there's no substitute for someone looking you in the eye and explaining how your job fits into the big picture.

First Interstate Bancorp is our parent corporation. It's the eleventh largest bank holding company in the country, covering the 13 western states and employing 33,000 people. First Interstate Bank of California, one of the four regional companies within the parent corporation, is comparable to a subsidiary, a strategic business unit or a business division; it's the fourth largest bank in California and has 13,000 employees.

At First Interstate, we strive for a coordinated communications program. We take video, face-to-face communications, and written communications and tie them all together so they reinforce the same messages and work to make the impact of those messages even stronger. We focus on business issues dealing with specific messages and business goals, which we constantly reinforce. We deal with multiple audiences, meaning different audiences geographically, exempt and non-exempt employees, and those in jobs ranging from credit officers to programmers to tellers in the local banks.

We concentrate on measuring results for two reasons: It helps keep us on the right track and allows for mid-course corrections. Second, quantitative, measured results explain our accomplishments very clearly to senior management.

Planning is a major priority. We begin our communications programs by determining audience and management needs, and then balancing the program to achieve both. We set objectives, themes and messages for a program, and provide input to the script in terms of ideas, language and use of numbers. We found that you need to keep concepts simple when you're talking to a wide audience.

Executives Face the "Troops"

All our face-to-face programs have three components: social/networking time, presentation of information, and an interactive question-and-answer session. We concentrate on preparing executives for question-and-answer segments. It takes a long time to convince some executives that it's okay to say, "I don't know the answer to your question, but I'll find out." We advise them to face the tough issues instead of dodging them.

We also try to provide feedback throughout a program to keep communication two-way, candid and relevant. For example, after the first meeting in a series of talks, we conduct phone surveys and then consult with executives to make mid-course corrections that enable them to make their presentations more effective in satisfying employees' needs.

Both qualitative and quantitative results are emphasized for the face-to-face programs. We conduct numerous phone surveys, and most of our programs have a brief quantitative written survey attached to them. In addition, our corporation conducts an employee attitude survey every two years, which includes 10 to 12 questions specifically dealing with communications and communications' vehicles.

Each year, we hold one or two senior management conferences on both the corporate and individual bank levels. Our corporate culture is also reinforced by emphasizing issues such as teamwork and customer service, which are very important to us. Holding one of these conferences at the corporate level in the first quarter of the year creates an information cascade down through the organization when individual banks then hold their own senior management conferences.

Another program at our California bank is called Calforums, which are basically large employee update meetings held three times a year. First, our corporate CEO goes out and talks about the corporation—the macro-view. Later in the year, the bank's CEO talks to about 18 different employee groups throughout California about the bank and its goals; and several months later, the bank's division managers speak about each division's goals and accomplishments. At least 3,000 employees attend each series and submit a multitude of questions, which we analyze according to the issues raised and provide feedback to senior management. We have a similar program at the Bancorp level; the 200 people in the corporate offices meet four times a year with the corporation's CEO. In addition, each year the corporation's CEO and the president visit all four regions of the corporation and talk with their management teams, at a minimum.

We have management advisory councils (MAC) in several regions, notably California and Texas. Members meet quarterly with the CEO and senior management, bringing questions from their major bank units; the answers are published in our "MAC Minutes." It's our job to make sure the questions receive solid answers. We also ask the MAC members to research big issues raised in the questions and to report back on progress and results.

Supporting Face-to-Face Communications

Video communications and telecommunications are also part of our face-to-face programs. Although these are not strictly face-to-face, they are similarly interactive. This technology allows us to disseminate one message simultaneously to all desired locations while maintaining a personal touch. We conducted our first video conference last spring, which was a two-hour, system-wide presentation and question-and-answer session to introduce a new credit program to credit officers. This program was followed by a half-hour meeting with the on-site senior managers at each of those 25 locations that received the transmission. This combination of video and face-to-face presentations proved to be very effective.

Two different programs illustrate our communications strategy. One at the bank level in California focused on achieving our 1985 five-year financial goal of a 1 percent return on assets (ROA). We developed a communications plan to heighten awareness of the goal using the coordinated approach mentioned earlier, with video and face-to-face meetings supplementing our written communications.

We tried to describe our goal of 1 percent ROA in a way that our tellers and customer service reps could understand. Our CEO, starting at the Calforums, explained 1 percent ROA with the example of a $100 profit on a $10,000 car loan. We then analyzed MAC and Calforum questions and viewpoint survey results to make sure we were on the right track. The program successfully increased employee awareness of our goals, thereby facilitating buy-in. By 1990 we had reached our goal of 1 percent ROA.

On the corporate level, our "corporate culture" goal is to get the whole institution thinking as one banking company, rather than as a company of banks. This is a major undertaking because we have so many branches, but we want to prepare for interstate banking. The corporation's CEO started explaining this philosophy at our senior management conference. To follow up, we then worked with our regional internal communications network—the internal communications people in all our regions—to reinforce the idea of acting as one unified company through a series of lower level meetings, a video, and subsequent newsletter and magazine articles. This program has made great progress during this first year.

Although our communications program has become increasingly effective over the past five years, there is still much more to do. As the environment, technology, and the needs of employees and the corporation change, so must communications.

Building Credibility for Increased Productivity

Nelson Farris
Director, Internal Relations
Nike, Inc.

Nike has some unique communications challenges. We must communicate with our 4,400 employees in the United States, as well as with global producers and distributors—an extremely diverse audience. About half of our people are under 29 years old; half are married; many of the singles are women with children; and approximately half of our employees are men. Length of service poses the most complex problem. In the last couple of years, we've hired about 2,000 employees. Managers have usually been around five years or more, while senior management has been around ten or more years. (We are 0 for 9 on outside executives; not one of them stuck.)

How do we get people to increase productivity? Employees have to believe in what you do. If they don't believe, they'll steal pencils and computers, and worse still, they'll mentally check out and just won't produce.

Our goal is to follow our corporate marketing style; the internal relations operation mimics what is done on the outside. We want to be innovative, aggressive, authentic and fun. Our goal is to inform employees before they hear about it in the news. We want to give them what we call "bragging rights." If your employees go home and talk about their work, you've got them because they have something they're proud of. They can share information—both the good and bad stuff—with friends and family because they know about it before it's on television or in the newspaper. That's very important.

Communicating the Culture

One handout we distribute at work is called "Instant Replay," a one-page flyer that gives topical information about Nike. Designed and named by employees, its goal is to record an event or speech, print it up, and get it distributed to all employees by that afternoon or the next day. Another example is called "Beyond the Berm," which is a one-page summary of "Nike in the News"—news from outside our corporate offices which takes about 30 seconds to read. (One of our mottoes is, "If you can't scan it, can it.") Both are globally distributed. Some of this stuff is on the edge; some of it's corny. We are a bit risky, but that's okay because it creates controversy and initiates dialogue.

We have "Brown Bag" sessions on campus to update employees about what's going on. Our human resources department sends out a "brown bag flyer" and invites you to bring your lunch to a session where we'll sit down and talk about some part of Nike. For example, one session was on the booming Nike women's line. We brought together all the women managers who run the business and invited the employees to hear them speak. It takes one hour and serves those who are interested. We do this as much as we can in all our locations around the world.

We have about 330 departments worldwide, and this fall we're asking each of them to produce a two-minute video about their department. This will be Nike's weirdest and funniest home videos. The mission is for our employees to tell us who they are and how they've contributed to Nike's successful year. We're taking Nike's values and asking everyone to use them in the production of their video: Be innovative, creative, get together as a team, do something you're proud of, and send it to us. We're going to edit these videos into one video and send it back to all departments so they can show their employees Nike's big picture and where they fit in the big picture.

We have road shows and corporate presentations. We did 30 one-hour presentations recently to explain some of our marketing campaigns. We explain our advertising, our shoes, apparel, and so on. We invite employees to come to these meetings and to participate. We'll package this show and take it to our customer service facilities in New Hampshire, Tennessee, Holland and Hong Kong.

We work with the training and development department on employee orientation. Employees learn what the company is all about, how we get things done, why we're successful, and what they have to do to keep us going for the next decade. It's not a one-time event but rather an ongoing education program.

We hold special events for employees which are tied into our corporate values and objectives, and we don't do them just because it's expected. For example, in July we had a huge picnic at the end of a long week celebrating diversity in the company. We served great food, had a band and the Nike beer relays—an old athletic event started in 1980. We turned this event into a 12-hour day. People brought the kids in the morning then took them home and came back for the evening entertainment. Two years ago we had a Christmas party in a huge tent; last Christmas we had no party, but we conducted a corporate giving campaign instead. We change our tune to suit the needs and feelings of the employees at the time.

We take advantage of our extraordinary connection to athletes. For example, Scottie Pippin of the Chicago Bulls visited the Nike home office. So we put some bleachers on the patio and got the CEO and a bunch of top executives together for a game of NIKE (like HORSE). Whenever an athlete visits us, we try to do something like this regardless of the location. We let our employees see our heroes. We fold people into the process of what's going on inside the company. These things add to your credibility.

We're trying to polarize a mix of diversity, ideas, culture and attitude to work together in "disorganized organization" without sacrificing quality. We're a "get in your face" company, and it works for Nike. If we help people believe in themselves, then they will believe in Nike. I encourage you to "just do it."

Designing a Successful Video Program

Catherine Chuplis
Corporate Video Manager
Levi Strauss & Company

If I had been asked to give advice on corporate video in 1985, I probably would have stressed intent, content and format: What you want to say, what your objectives are, who your intended audience is, and what format is best. Despite the different formats of the 1980s, I would have said, "Remember to be suggestive, not exhaustive. Use a linear format. Your audience won't sit and watch your video for very long because your audience is video literate; they watch television every night."

Much has changed since 1985, and in the 1990s I recommend looking into the future and anticipating where video design is going. The most significant fact about the future of video is the merging of computers with television. That means that we're no longer going to be a passive audience, sitting back watching without interaction (a linear format). People will be able to interact and choose how much they want to learn. In essence, it's a power shift from the transmitter (the video department passing out the various messages) to the receiver or audience who is able to interact.

In the video of the 1990s, we've got to be suggestive in the linear pieces but exhaustive in terms of what somebody might want to know. They may want to know a little, or they may want greater detail. In organizations of the future, where employees are empowered, this really fits in. The interactive design is the empowering design. The work station of the future will enable an individual to find out what they want to know; "tell me more" will be the phrase of the future. As we push decision-making down in our organizations, the need to supply people with information in greater and greater detail with interactive design will be increasingly critical. Now, most of us have PCs at our desk, but it won't be long before we're going to have multimedia capabilities.

Working on the Future Today

Since this technology is not here yet, Levi Strauss has attempted to simulate that kind of interactive system and has begun to get people to ask, "How can I learn more?" One of our experiments is a linear video called *The Global Forum* which asks questions about our company's business strategy but does not directly provide answers. Rather, it helps employees understand the global strategic business plan at Levi Strauss. It's broken into three segments, with discussion time in between. Study tapes focus on specific aspects of the discussion.

Our attempts to stimulate dialogue between the executive managers and the bottom of the company have been extremely effective. People are asking questions and are interested in what's going on. We don't use high-end production, and this vehicle changes every time we try to raise discussion about another strategic element of our global business plan. It's always accompanied by printed material because it can go into greater detail. It also has a discussion guide for managers.

Our distribution system created waves, too. Because the project is funded by the executive management committee, they tried to use their clout to push the video down in the organization; that didn't work. So we started a bottom-up campaign; we asked people if they'd seen the video yet, and if not, why they were being denied access to this information. It worked! People went to their managers and asked to see the video.

The interactive design will require decentralization of a video unit. The future will demand that we all interface over video, but because it's a cold medium, people need practice with it. We're identifying people around the company who have some basic presentation skills and are comfortable in front of a camera. Five years ago, I would have said never to use real employees in the videos, but people are less concerned with "smooth and high-tech" now.

We've started pilots around the company. For example, we supply people with VHS cameras and tripods, and we send out video specialists to train people on Video 101 techniques. They're actually producing videos and sending them to us. We use the videos to let other employees know what's going on around the company, and we share these videos with contractors and suppliers to help them work better with us.

As we move from the industrial era into the age of communications, the demand for visual information is going to grow. If we're going to be effective as video communicators, we need to think of how to design interactively so that we're poised and ready for the next generation of PCs.

Part III

Managing the Communications Process

Phyllis Piano
Manager, Communications & Community Relations
General Electric Medical Systems

General Electric Medical Systems is a $3 billion subsidiary of General Electric; it's the world leader in diagnostic imaging. All our competitors are global companies—Siemens, Toshiba, Philips. We have three regional headquarters in Paris, Tokyo and Milwaukee, with additional offices all over. The time difference among these three regions make person-to-person communications difficult, particularly during a crisis.

Different Regions, Different Needs

Different areas have different communications needs. In the Americas, we had major reorganizations creating a workload crunch. We had people who'd never been out of the United States traveling all over the world trying to integrate a new business. Canada and Latin America were telling us not to forget about them.

Back in 1988, the morale in Europe was terrible. The prevailing attitude was that they were taken over by "big GE," and there were scores of layoffs and consolidations. They had no formal communication plans; newsletters and informative meetings were just starting. Not long after the acquisition, we did a survey in Europe that showed some severe attitude problems due to the downsizing, but the marks in communication were up dramatically. People admitted that, while they didn't necessarily like what they were hearing, GE improved communication, and they now knew more of what was going on.

In Asia, where there was plenty of growth and opportunities, the challenges were dramatically different. We just started a new organization to coordinate our Asian efforts. The Japanese joint venture communicated very well, but timing was a problem. We also now have joint ventures in India, China and other countries.

The question was how to link all this together around the world. Our senior vice president suggested a worldwide communication task force. This group, of which I am a member, had three face-to-face meetings, first in Tokyo, then in Paris, and last in the United States. We purposely did the United States last to emphasize that our other locations were just as important.

We needed mechanisms to make announcements around the world. We looked at:

- *Training:* Do our managers know how to communicate?
- *Recognition:* How does it differ from country to country?
- *Communications mediums:* Can the same medium work in the United States and in France?
- *Communication planning:* How can we work together to communicate similar themes and messages?
- *Measurements:* How do we know that it's working?

Plans We Implemented

It was easy to translate the major stories from the world publication, which is distributed to all 15,000 employees, into Japanese and French. This is done through our global network at no cost; they simply send us a disc. It gives the majority of employees a chance to read what's going on in their own language. It also emphasizes to our employees, particularly in the United States, that we are a global business.

Within our group, we instantly communicate important announcements to the entire business through paper or electronic mail. Our global network shares information and decides whether it should go out globally or regionally. I serve as a lead, and we work together on what should be distributed where. One of the more difficult tasks is to coordinate our communication plans so that leaders of the Americas, Asia and Europe have consistent themes and messages. We worked on this in the task force and came up with a plan.

We've made a lot of progress in measurement. Every major communication effort is tracked. For example, our goal was to communicate to all employees within 48 hours that the leader in Europe had changed. We found that in Asia 67 percent of those surveyed knew in 48 hours; in the Americas, 74 percent knew.

Another communication tool is the quarterly management meetings held in the different regions, hosted by our global leaders. Using continuous improvement techniques, we change the format to satisfy the participants, but we still have a long way to go. The information from the meetings is shared through the communications network.

To get a read on attitudes in communication, we are going to conduct a global attitude survey early in 1992, which will be translated into 11 languages. For a long time, GE has been doing attitude surveys, but we've never given everyone the same questions (altered only for culture) at the same time. It's a huge undertaking that involves giving detailed feedback to all our employees.

One of the ways we stay integrated is to have an annual management meeting among communications groups. We take this opportunity to package the communication from the meeting and finalize our communication plans for the year. One of the keys to success was getting to know each other by meeting face-to-face and becoming a team, which is not easy when you're dealing with different cultures and norms. We also tried to take the best from each part of the world and share it; this way everybody wins.

Can We Influence European Governments?

Andrew A. Napier
Director, Governmental & Corporate Affairs
Ford of Europe Inc.

I am a director of governmental and corporate affairs, an area involving more than just work done by specialists. Although we do have specialists at the head office and at most of the national companies, the most important governmental affairs work is often done by the chairman or the managing director, with the governmental affairs staff there to help them.

Our job is to provide 5- to 10-year planning assumptions and to ensure that consistent planning assumptions are used throughout the corporation. It's nice if the assumptions are right, but it's more important that they be consistent across the board. We analyze the impact of events or likely scenarios and help develop the appropriate strategy. We are also responsible for insuring that action is taken both internally and externally. This can work the other way around as well: If business development managers have a particular project, they will come to us and ask whether or not what they have proposed will work, or if it would best be done slightly differently.

Using Information Strategically

In the complicated European Community (EC) environment, the real secret is to strike a balance between information and action. If you spend too much time and effort on information gathering and analysis, you probably won't have enough time for action. This probably won't do your company much good—or much harm. On the other hand, some governmental affairs people devote too much time to action and not enough time to gathering information and analyzing the impact. This *can* be dangerous if the action is irrelevant. Corporate credibility is likely to suffer, and the company's reputation may be at stake.

A governmental affairs manager has three basic responsibilities:

- understand the organization's objectives, priorities, plans, strengths and weaknesses;
- understand the business environment; and
- prioritize and manage resources.

Governmental affairs people need to stand back occasionally to anticipate and prepare for possible events. It's a little like a juggling act: You've got to keep several issues in the air at one time but then prioritize.

What sort of issues does your company have? Is an issue company-specific or industry-specific? Does it affect other industries as well? If so, maybe the Confederation of Industries of the European Community (UNICE), which unites the interest of all industries, can help. If you can say, "This affects all industries, but we have a company-specific viewpoint," you'll need to work specifically on behalf of your own organization as well as work through an industry association.

The Complicated EC Government Structure

With the coming of the EC, life became more complex for governmental affairs people. In national governments, it's relatively easy to discover which ministers and officials are interested and influential in particular issues. On the EC level, Brussels is not the be all and end all; the European Council (all heads of national governments) is taking on an increasingly important role. The Council of Ministers (national government ministers) effectively makes the key decisions based on proposals made by the Commission, which has different layers all with different roles. The Committee of Permanent Representatives (COREPER)—sort of national ambassadors to the EC—also has an important role in Brussels. The European Court of Justice in Luxembourg is arguably the most important body of all.

In the European Parliament, members have Europe-wide responsibility but are nationally elected. The Economic and Social Committee is also nationally appointed. There are many more people involved in the governing process, and each has a different role to play.

Choose Your Battles (and Allies) Wisely

Obviously, you can't change everything. You also need to look for overlapping interests and to build bridges between your own interests and those of others. If you can think of your own organization as a part of a larger system, it will be easier to concentrate on the part of your universe that you will be able to influence.

Realize that your actions do leave a specific impression. Many people overlook this fact. Is your criticism constructive, or are you just complaining? If you make a particular point on an issue, what's your hidden message? For example, I will consciously look for opportunities to publicly support European integration because we want it, the Commission and most peole in "Brussels" want it, and even though "Brussels" sometimes comes up with some crazy ideas, we don't want to just be seen as spoilers.

The message underlying key points is absolutely vital because all our lobbying tells decision-makers and opinion leaders something about our organization. If they hear us only when we're complaining, they see us only as complainers. If you discuss your objectives, what you think would actually help, what you think is the best way of achieving your common objectives, perhaps you can create a productive dialogue.

We shouldn't just lobby people; we must *talk* to them. We must build an ongoing relationship of trust with all the various people out there whose interests may overlap ours and whose actions can affect the way we do business in the European Community—and the world.

Organizing Cross-Cultural Communications

Thomas Henderson
Director of Communications
Dow Europe S.A.

Dow Chemical is the sixth largest chemical company in the world. Plastics, chemicals and performance products are our major business, but we also produce consumer specialties such as pharmaceuticals, DowBrands and agricultural chemicals. Dow Europe, which includes 32 manufacturing locations, 67 sales offices, and nine major research companies, generates about one-third of the sales of the total company.

Dow Europe's communications is split into three groups:

- *Region communications* handles internal and external communications (employee and corporate) on a day-to-day basis and during a crisis. Across Europe we have nine major headquarters for these groups.
- *Marketing communications* promotes plastics, chemicals and performance products, but not pharmaceuticals, the agriculture business, or the DowBrands business. (These last three operate as separate profit centers.)
- The *core group* in Switzerland essentially helps the people in regional communications by producing position papers, by making sure that the Dow Europe messages are accurate, and by acting as a support agency. If a regional initiative is suitable in a given case, we make sure they take it.

Culture Dictates the Medium

Like many large multinationals, we have a cultural communications problem. It's becoming increasingly difficult for corporate communications to deemphasize the importance of national identity while recognizing and respecting national pride. In addition, employee differences in job status, education, age, sex, politics and religion also hinder communications. We've found in many instances that we cannot use American-style written communications or videotape in the United Kingdom, no less translate them from American to French. Acquisitions and joint ventures also pose a particular set of problems: It takes a long time to get the experience and the confidence of any new organization, even with adequate communications.

We value employee communications; it's not just a sideline of human resources. In many companies, it receives no funds and isn't supported by a professional staff or adequate research. The wrong tools are used to tell employees what the company wants to tell them and not what they really need to know.

At Dow, we've tried to delegate responsibility for most employee communications to the regions. Again, what works in one culture may not necessarily work in another. We find that some cultures read more than others and are more interested in corporate information; others prefer visuals. For example, we've had great success with video in the manufacturing locations, but none with the snippets of news we put out every two months. The regional communications people know the local culture best, so we give them the opportunity to decide how the employees in their region get information from the company and what sort of information they want.

The success of distribution methods can also vary by target audience. We've tried sending the latest internal communications to employees' homes. The success of this varies by culture. Some really enjoy it, especially Germans; others, such as Italians, don't want to be bothered at home.

To quickly communicate management changes or important information, we have tried using computer screens. The drawback: People like pictures to be included, but screens can't provide this at present.

Our employees still prefer the personal touch. We've been very successful with getting more executives to talk with employees and reinforce video messages. We've still got to convince executives of the importance of getting out there and doing live presentations. These impress upon employees the importance of a particular piece of news. If the executives believe our people are the most important asset to the company, they should show that through personal appearances.

Cross-Cultural Successes

Some projects do cut across cultures well, however. Employees are interested in topics they're involved with. For example, our greatest success has been an ambassador newsletter. Environmental information is disseminated, so employees can act as ambassadors on issues that Dow has a position on.

We're also finding that creating messages for specific groups is effective. For instance, we have about 140 people working in the packaging industry across Europe. Seventy-five percent of these employees drive a considerable amount, so we use audio tape. We incorporate requested music along with the messages, in order to make the tapes interesting, informative and interactive.

Granted, there's no hard and fast rule, but we're putting extra time and effort into every communications opportunity we get. Our standards are high, and we strive to present clear, proper messages. We have learned that different information requires different strategies and that communications is an ongoing process.

Employee Communications Across Cultural Borders

Felix Bjorklund
*Vice President, Communications &
External Programs
IBM Europe S.A.*

IBM Europe has a little more than 100,000 employees at the moment. Our revenue last year was $27 billion making us the largest business unit in IBM. Ninety-five percent of the revenue comes from 17 European countries. IBM Europe handles manufacturing, marketing, and research and development. In addition, we are opening offices in most of the Eastern European countries and the Soviet Union, and we are trying a new organizational structure, IBM Nordic.

Even though IBM has been operating in Europe for a long time and IBM employees have "IBM thinking," cultures and values differ across Europe. We also see language barriers within our company. This means that employee communications cannot rely on one language or similar messages.

However, it's imperative that each employee act as a corporate ambassador to spread the vision of the company. They must understand what is going on. This requires consistent information across the company, across cultures, and across borders in both external and internal communications, including advertising and promotions. Timing is the key: Employees should read about company news before it gets to the press.

Getting Out a Message

Our framework is such that we develop an overall European communications plan once a year and update it as necessary. We look at the European business environment within our industry and IBM Europe's business plan. This helps us to ascertain where IBM Europe wants to go and where the challenges are. From this, we decide how internal and external communications can support the business directions of the company. We develop a set of communications actions and messages that we want to consistently promote.

Developing a plan may be easy, but "selling" a single message isn't. There is no real European press, and few countries even have country-wide papers. Major magazines have circulations of only a few hundred thousand. The same is true for television: There have been many attempts at developing European commercial channels, but none has been very successful. Clearly, investments will grow in both public and private networks, but we are not there yet.

IBM has two worldwide communications tools: An English magazine called *Think* and a management briefing. A couple of people in Europe make sure that European stories and news get in *Think*. Its circulation in Europe totals 50,000—approximately half of all employees.

Within Europe, we tried a European magazine which was distributed to 20,000 employees. However, individual countries have their own employee magazines, management packages, meetings, and experimental videotapes and television. We dropped it because we were simply duplicating information and running into language barriers. It was also an impossible task to get people to read all the publications. Now, we write a number of articles focusing on 10 European issues. These articles are sent to the countries, which translate them and put them into their local magazines.

In addition, we have an information management package that goes out four times a year to European managers. They choose the material they want, so we're not forcing countries to accept publications they can't use due to language problems. Instead, we give them input to include in their local communications.

Up-and-Coming Technology

We have experimented with new media. We have an internal computer network to which all employees have access, so we're using that more. For example, in most countries we've moved bulletin boards onto the screen. That allows us to get out information such as European-level bulletins quickly: Send it to a country, translate it, and then distribute it. That's how to cover urgent, internal messages.

We have also experimented with television. It worked well in the United States, but a couple of problems arose in Europe. First, technical problems still exist; standards are not fixed. Second are language barriers. You can't centralize European programming. You need separate country networks and programs which cover European-wide issues, making investment costs very high.

New technology is evolving, called "PC Multimedia," which will allow television programming to be sent through an internal network. We have opted against implementing this right now; instead, we want to launch a regular video program to accustom people to seeing the news on television instead of reading it. This will complement the European magazines and improve the use of the internal network. Europe-wide, we produce six video news programs per year that are sent to the various countries. These come in two forms: a complete program, usable "as is"; and news that can be translated and incorporated into country video programming.

All communications is designed to inform people of the challenges facing us. We use both internal and external people to give credibility to the programs, and we try to be open in the dialogue.

The Changing World and Satellite Communications

Bruce L. Crockett
President & Chief Executive Officer
COMSAT Corporation

I'd like to take a basic, pragmatic look at the satellite business and COMSAT's future in it. Mobil communications will soon be our largest business. People want to communicate wherever they are—even from ships, cars and remote locations. Aeronautical communications is also taking off. In 1990, we began cockpit data service to commercial airliners; this year, we'll expand our agreement with GTE Airphone to include service on international flights. With Sony Transcom, we'll offer in-flight news service. Whatever business executives do on the ground, they'll soon be able to do in the air.

The demand for the transmission of news, business, and sporting events over satellites seems insatiable. Next year, INTELSAT will launch a new satellite called the INTELSAT K, which will enable broadcasters to use smaller, less expensive Earth stations for reception. When the time comes, the K SAT, as it's often called, will be ready for high definition television and digital audio radio. The INTELSAT 7 satellites, the next generation, will start to go up in 1992. They will carry data and television traffic and will be able to respond to regional growth by shifting capacity to wherever it's needed most.

Consulting Services and Global Joint Ventures

We're also going to focus on businesses which are not capital intensive and complement what we already do. We're enthusiastic about our consulting, engineering and systems integration business. These value-added services pull together our capabilities and the reputation of our labs on a worldwide basis for delivery to both governments and commercial customers.

We're also tuned into the idea of international joint ventures. The worldwide trend towards privatization of state-owned telecommunications companies has opened tremendous opportunities. We're working on projects in more than a dozen countries. In Latin America within the last 18 months, we've set up joint ventures in Venezuela, Argentina, Chile and Guatemala, providing domestic and international private line services. More ventures will be announced soon. As the Latin economies grow, more opportunities will be created for us. In Eastern Europe and the former Soviet Union, we're partners in a joint venture that will bring wireless cable television to 26 million people in 13 different markets. Using our specific expertise, COMSAT Video Enterprise will be beaming these signals all over the world.

We're also developing new market segments. For example, in some areas, the traditional heavy route traffic is going to decline because of fiber optic cables. To make up for this migration to cables, we're concentrating on those areas where satellites are better. We're building new markets in parts of the world not readily served by cable, such as Latin America and Eastern Europe. There's a new, segmented world out there that cable can't easily serve.

We're a globally oriented company in a global age. Our emphasis is on a new vision and new value. We are not restricting ourselves, nor are we resting on our laurels or depending on the protections of the past. COMSAT is looking forward to the future. We're prepared, and we can't wait for it to arrive.

Part IV

Attempted Merger at Southern California Edison

Lewis M. Phelps
Vice President - Corporate Communication
Southern California Edison Company

In the summer of 1988, San Diego Gas & Electric (SDG&E) proposed a merger with Tucson Electric Power Company in Arizona, which effectively put SDG&E in play by pricing their company. Our finance people believed that Southern California Edison could do better for SDG&E shareholders, so we proposed an alternative merger. We filed requests for approval with the Public Utilities Commission in San Francisco and with the Federal Energy Regulatory Commission in Washington, D.C.; it took two full years before the regulators decided against the merger.

During those two years, we were in the San Diego press—frequently front-page news—almost every day. The publisher of *The San Diego Union* and *The San Diego Tribune* was a close friend of the mayor, and they jointly decided that they wanted to fight this merger. Reporters from these publications have told us they were under explicit orders to intensively cover the merger with a very pronounced negative slant.

Our problems started with a series of mistaken assumptions. We assumed that we would have public support in San Diego because we could cut the electric rates for customers by about 40 percent. That turned out to be false. In fact, although bashing SDG&E had been a favorite sport of both the local media and politicians for several decades, all the local critics of SDG&E rallied against the merger.

We didn't count on such a strong anti-Los Angeles attitude among San Diego residents, either. Local politicians and media banded with the labor unions representing SDG&E's employees, the Utilities Consumers' Action Network (UCAN), the downtown business community, and environmentalists. We assumed that this coalition wouldn't stick together because there were so many divergent interests within it—another wrong assumption.

Most important, Southern California Edison enjoys a reputation in the area we serve as a credible, stable, well-managed and well-performing company with a strong community interest. We assumed that our reputation would carry over to San Diego. It did not. Our reputation in San Diego was colored from the outset by the media coverage and by the anti-Los Angeles attitude. We were cast as a big Los Angeles company coming in to take over the local San Diego utility. (In fact, we don't even serve the city of Los Angeles.) Unfortunately, we made all these assumptions without ever testing them, and they ended up hurting us.

Action for Improving Public Perceptions

We finally got a clear idea of where we were headed and what kind of problems we had, and accomplished a number of things that helped us turn around the public opinion climate somewhat. First and most important, public relations was very much involved in the decision-making process. This allowed us to discuss the public relations implications of certain actions and advise the lawyers, in particular, on what steps to take.

Second, it was very helpful to obtain good outside public relations counsel. We hired a San Diego PR firm to represent us even though we have a large internal public relations organization. Their counsel was invaluable because they provided knowledge about the local attitudes; connections to the political arena in San Diego; and an objective, third-party viewpoint of our actions.

We took a number of polls in San Diego during the course of the merger. The polling was helpful in guiding our actions. For example, it showed that our credibility among the people of San Diego was so low that paid advertising wasn't worth the money. So we developed an alternative strategy of third-party endorsements, which helped to offset negative attitudes.

Next, we spoke with a consistent voice during the entire crisis. I was the sole media spokesman. When I was unavailable, my second in command took over. We also had the company's chairman speak from time to time, but that was it. We use one spokesperson in a crisis for one simple reason: I know what I've said and don't have to worry about someone else having said something different, which could allow people to accuse us of changing our story. In our two years under intensive media scrutiny, nothing we said came back to haunt us.

It's really important to monitor what the media are saying. It is very easy for reporters to use clips as references. This means that if you see something wrong in one story, you have to get it corrected in every reporter's clip files. In our San Diego situation, one reporter, Charlie Ross of *The San Diego Union,* set the tone for everything written or said about the merger. The broadcast media in particular simply picked up what Ross said and reiterated it. So if we saw a Charlie Ross story that had an error in it, we were on the phone within minutes talking to the television stations to make sure they didn't repeat that error, at least not without hearing our side.

Finally, in a crisis situation, adopt allies wherever you can find them. In San Diego, our allies came almost exclusively from two categories of people: minority organizations and labor unions. Those are the last two classes of organizations that you'd expect an electric utility to win as allies. In fact, we were viewed by those groups as an opportunity for change in San Diego because we have a reputation of being very open and positive toward working with minority vendors.

The key elements of effective management of the communications process are frequent and open communication, and making sure you spread the same message to all audiences. The message has got to be consistent and timely. Unfortunately, even if you do all that, you're probably still going to be "behind the eight ball" because reporters are generally more interested in a sexy story than a good story.

Addressing Safety and Environmental Issues

Thomas Houston
Manager, Media Relations
Chrysler Corporation

Recently, I conducted some very rigorous and objective research to determine what kind of animal public relations professionals think newspeople are. The results were astonishing: 80 percent of public relations professionals surveyed said the animal most like a journalist is a duck. The "press duck" has webbed feet for stomping all over press releases, stubby wings to fly from perception to unsupported conclusion, oily feathers to keep the deluge of facts from penetrating, and dim eyes for seeing past today into tomorrow and maybe next week. Most important, he has a toothed bill for nibbling public relations people to death. Dealing with the media today is a lot like being nibbled to death by a duck.

Nowhere is that more apparent than when you're seeking fair and appropriate coverage on environmental and safety issues. I don't think the press is interested in fair and appropriate news as we see it. Instead, they prefer balance, which means calling a corporation (meaning an environmental ogre) on one side of an issue to get a quote and then calling someone on the other side of the issue to get a quote. They call this a news story. This doesn't mean you will lose all your safety and environmental battles in the media, but the wins are going to be hard fought.

At Chrysler, we've been on both sides of the environmental battle. Sometimes the media see us as good guys and sometimes as bad guys. Chrysler is paying for the sins of our previous generation because literally hundreds of stories are out there waiting for that press duck to nibble Chrysler to death: the sludge at a new apartment complex in Michigan, built on what was Chrysler property; a farm in Wisconsin where an employee dumped pink sludge and solvents; and an old stamping plant in Detroit. Each of these has the potential of becoming a page-one horror story; in fact, some of them have.

We took a lot of flack at first on these issues, but by and large were able to deflect the press duck by being upright, up-front and forthright. We took the story to the media and didn't wait for the media to come to us. We have many experts at Chrysler on matters of safety and environment; after a couple of disasters, they turned into an early warning system for us in media relations. They now warn us when they learn about something coming down the pike. This helps us considerably because we can get ready before that duck gets loose.

The "Return" of the Pink Sludge

In that Wisconsin incident, the environmental people kept us apprised every step of the way. The result is that we went to the residents before the guys in the moon suits showed up drilling holes in somebody's lawn. An employee who owned the business before Chrysler bought it was contracted to haul away the 55-gallon barrels of junk. He took hundreds of these barrels home and dumped them in a ravine at the back of his farm. He was being paid to dispose of these things legally; he did not. In the process, he contaminated the groundwater. We learned about the problem when one of his neighbors complained to the Wisconsin authorities, who told our environmental personnel, who then came to us. That's when our guys in moon suits showed up in Wisconsin. We had to do something to clean up that mess, and we had to find out what it was all about.

After we gathered as many facts as possible, we laid our cards on the table. We went to the government officials in the area and told them that we wanted to hold a public meeting because we wanted to reassure the people affected and wanted to talk about the problem. The government agreed, and they informed the media of the meeting. The media became our conduit to talk to the residents; we were trying to do good, so the media gave us a break on the story. The story lead concentrated on the fact that the farm was contaminated, but it also said that Chrysler Corporation was doing something about it. We held two other public meetings in which we let the residents say what they wanted on how they felt about this problem. We tested the water of anyone who was concerned (we still do). And we are constructing an $80 million facility on the property to decontaminate the water and literally cook the soil to get the contaminants out before we dump the soil back in place. We even tested the local crops for contamination.

We started out as bad guys in Wisconsin, but our image is getting better all the time. We learned that you can diffuse some of these disasters by being honest, open, accurate and early. If you are all of these, the press duck will not be as likely to nip at your toes. In fact, you can prevent the press duck from nibbling at your toes by force-feeding it a big serving of the truth.

Communications' Role in Redefining a Culture

Richard M. Madden
Director, Internal Communications
Allstate Insurance Company

Like many companies, Allstate is facing social, political and economic change. To survive, it needed a culture change. As a result, Allstate introduced the vision and values, made up of several components: a mission, four commitments, and four basic values.

Since we were asked to communicate vision and values without creating a new program, we consciously developed a strategy that would work over the long haul, filled with subtlety. We identified six key channels (executive speeches, support materials, corporate publications, local publications, telecasting and research) to execute our plan.

Executive speeches were the most critical tactic in the introduction and initial definition of the vision. The aim was to build consensus among management personnel—roughly 7,000 people. The vision was introduced in 1989 at the annual chairman's conference. First, he defined the values, mission and commitments, tempering those three definitions by stating that these were only initial definitions and that the vision was flexible, based on employee feedback and company performance. The importance of the chairman's words were underscored when his speech was telecast to every manager in the company coast to coast. Every leader received the new "rules" at the same time and from the same person. The executive speech continues to play a key role in advancing our vision, values and commitments.

High Visibility Spreads the Word

At the beginning of 1990, each employee received support materials aimed at bringing the vision closer to them and their jobs. Each employee received a prism to keep on his or her desk as a reference when a question arose about what to do or how to behave in any given situation. The chairman considered this the company manual. As a company that was used to committees and going through bureaucratic layers to get an answer, this was a big departure for us.

Each employee also received a business card with the vision on it, which many officers kept in a shirt pocket or wallet. If they were trying to make a point in a meeting, it could be pulled out and discussed. In each conference room there is a framed plaque with basically the same thing. With time, it keeps coming into the culture and is used as a reference. If anyone argues against your point, it is very difficult for them to win the argument when you have this on your side.

Corporate publications' role in the introduction, development and continuing definition of the vision is significant. In fact, they became the work horse of the entire communication effort. Shortly after the vision was introduced, the *Bottom Line*—one of our publications for managers—featured the vision and reiterated the chairman's address. *Leaders,* our new management newsletter, keeps hammering away exactly what the vision means for this management group.

We continue to feature stories that deal with our values and commitments in every edition of our corporate-wide magazine. We also help to reinforce the concepts behind the values: caring, integrity, initiative and innovation. In addition, corporate publications connect our vision to the everyday business strategies.

While change is evolutionary, we believe that it has direction as well as focus. A clear corporate strategy, communicated to all employees, may mean the difference between dying and surviving in the 1990s.

Molding Communications to The Organization

Tricia E. Palermo
Director, Corporate Communications
Pacific Telesis Group

In the late 1970s, Pacific Telephone was a political football between AT&T (its parent) and the California Public Utilities Commission. Pacific's 112,000 employees were considered part of the sick child of the Bell System. In 1980, AT&T sent Donald Guinn, their network engineering vice president, to be the chairman of Pacific Telephone.

Guinn and the management team saw that there would be tremendous change and a need for new thinking in the management pool. Guinn's analogy at the time was that taking Pacific Telephone and turning it into Pacific Telesis was like taking apart a 747 in flight, rearranging it, and putting it back together without spilling any coffee on the passengers. The not spilling any coffee is the most important part.

Guinn's management team, which was formed in order to prepare for divestiture, divided itself into functional areas. There was a function called "communications" in charge of renaming the company, launching a new advertising look to identify the new company, deciding which company values were going to be retained and which would be changed, and handling a highly paternalistic and family-oriented culture. The strategic planners decided that communications would hold the same importance in the business plan as other functional areas like asset management and labor unions.

Something Old; a lot of New

Guinn and his direct reports did some communicating, too. They set out on a speaking tour that included every place they could get invited. Guinn went to Congress, state legislatures and employee groups to say that we were going to make the financials better. It was as truthful as could be. Officers speaking for themselves has always been a Bell tradition, and these folks continued it.

Some market-driven principles were overlaid on this base. In addition to knowing the internal audience, it became important to know the competition. Who else was drawing people's attention or saying anything that we would need to counter, disprove or overcome? Suddenly, all the normal tools such as video, publications and speeches weren't enough. It became very important to use the grapevine to contribute to the information flow. Officers used to ignore the grapevine, but if the grapevine worked, they were willing to use it, too.

The reorganization also changed the way the communications function worked. Since we couldn't hire enough inside staff, we had to buy expertise for the short term and be cost-efficient with it. We also learned to react quickly to changing conditions and to hold high expectations. Part of the planning process at that time was an acknowledgment that we *couldn't* plan for everything and that much of what we were going to do would be ad hoc and quick.

All this happened in the framework of the vision set by Guinn and this team: We are going to turn Pacific Telephone into a world-class telecommunications company. To do that, they had to prove to everybody—internal and external—that the financial job could be done. They had to convince AT&T to assume $1 billion of debt that was on Pacific Telephone's books prior to divestiture. That negotiation was highly publicized in the financial press. Pacific was playing hard ball, and I remember hearing fellow employees say that maybe we would pull this off after all. From then on, every decision that was publicized in the business press became fodder for the internal mill as well. To this day, any news for the media is also an employee communication.

Special vehicles were selected in the new corporation's early years to illustrate the vision, like the America's Cup in San Francisco and the L.A. Olympics. The tactical work done throughout the period was not unusual: newsletters, company magazines, video, officer meetings, letter-writing back and forth, electronic mail, and so on. What is important is that we've used every possible resource since then.

Every couple of years, we send out surveys to understand how messages are being received within and across subsidiary boundaries. Another gauge of our success in communication is audience response. We have had to shut down, sell or merge some businesses we started in 1984 and 1985, but there has not been one lawsuit, no employee backlash, and no financial community backlash. Communications have been managed so people understand a long time in advance what we're doing and why we're doing it.

Mistakes Help Us Grow

Of course, we haven't handled everything well. Once we failed to check with the employees of the largest subsidiary about whether or not they wanted a new leadership program. We simply gave them one and ordered them to go. They rebelled and complained, but management didn't respond. So someone called the press and that resulted in a hefty fine from the California Public Utilities Commission for using our phone bill money to support this training program. It's not that the idea was wrong; we simply didn't communicate well and didn't listen when people tried to tell us so.

In 1984, we didn't tell management employees about negotiations to sell one of our new subsidiaries. Non-management employees found out about it from their union friends. Again, the leak went to the press because we hadn't told our own folks what we were doing. Negotiating the sale of a company causes unfortunate incidents—like the Securities Exchange Commission shaking its finger at you about disclosure.

And one time we were trying to retrain employees to be more aggressive marketers, but they felt they were being asked to deceive the customer. Once again, non-management employees in the union reacted very strongly and went to the press. There needed to be a correction.

We're not perfect, but we're trying hard to make sure that we retain some of the traditional culture of our company yet integrate new practices where appropriate. Today, the message is, "Keep communicating, keep listening, keep trying when you don't succeed, stay flexible, and stay very focused on your business."

Sending a Positive Message During Difficult Times

Terrence D. Straub
Vice President, Public Affairs
USX Corporation

Most of the articles in today's business magazines are hardly sensational. The major role of the business press is to inform, and it does an increasingly good job at it. There is no imperative in the media to hound or to embarrass. Corporations shouldn't be timid in their public pronouncements or intimidated when put in a less-than-favorable light. But sending a believable, positive message during difficult times requires sending well-articulated, positive messages all the time. In other words, it's an ongoing strategy, not a one-time crisis response.

At USX, we've enjoyed an arm's-length friendship with both the local and national business press. This has been tried and tempered, and there has been no free ride for either side. Nor has there been any attempt by us to purposely deceive or by them to act irresponsibly.

Our chairman, Chuck Corry, holds four media conferences a year whether there's any special news or not. It gives the print and broadcast people an opportunity to ask anything that's on their minds. He does it out of Pittsburgh, where our corporate headquarters is located, but reporters in Houston, also a significant location, are linked so that both local press can pose questions. The national media send folks to Pittsburgh. Such a tradition goes a long way toward dispelling the notion that we're hiding something or that we only go public when it's to our advantage or we have something to brag about.

That's an important part of a strategy when it comes to handling a crisis. Our U.S. Steel plant outside Philadelphia was cited by the Occupational Safety and Health Administration a few years ago for safety violations. It was a big story in *The Philadelphia Inquirer*, and it was reported in a highly inflammatory misleading fashion. Rather than let the matter fester or imply that the article was true by silence, we responded strongly. Our chairman wrote a vigorous reply to the paper outlining our position and criticizing the paper's hyperbole. In addition, we took out a full-page ad in that paper and reprinted the letter. We think this cooled a hot situation, and we garnered some respect as a company that was not going to be bullied by the press.

Our greatest asset was the chairman, who toured the plant in question unannounced before issuing the letter. He did this to satisfy in his own mind that we were telling the truth when we responded to the allegations. His credibility was at the heart of our ability to respond forcefully. The story died two days later.

When we find ourselves needing the press to explain our position in a difficult time, we can't realistically expect favors, only a fair shake. Most of the time, if we've been open, available and honest in the quiet times, we won't have to fear the media in times of distress.